NOT
QUITE
HEAVEN

Not Quite Heaven

Poems

Ricardo Moran

BROKEN TRIBE PRESS

Not Quite Heaven

Paperback ISBN: 9781965412183

Front cover art and design by Jacob Arms

Published by Broken Tribe Press
Lawrence Landing Company
Raleigh, North Carolina 27609
USA, North America

Broken Tribe Press is a proud member of:

Independent Book Publishers Association
 and
Community of Literary Magazines and Presses

www.brokentribepress.com

BROKEN TRIBE PRESS

DEDICATION

For my husband, Jim Martin.
Te amo.

Para Santa Cecilia.
Muchísimas gracias.

CONTENTS

Dystopia Rules

Dystopia Threatened

Dystopia Fights Back

Dystopia Collapses

Aftermath

Utopia Ascends

Dystopia Rules

It arrived in light
this magician of words
who turned mirrors
into revolving doors,
into windowless windows,
and made you think
that this was real.

Blue Light Special

This flat, heat-soaked town
has a spinning blue light
keeping watch in a store.

Perched on a silver pole,
fused to a silver cart,
it looks like it could take me
to the future,
but it just sits there.

And in 1981,
I knew of no one like me
who cringed
when he held hands with a girl.

And I didn't know
I had the right to say no.

As this blue light turns, it draws shoppers
to trinkets in bins, to stacked bedsheets,
mesmerized eyes on discount towels.

Quietly, I pick up a pack of men's briefs
because I was 10 and that's all there was.

My hand traces the smiling white man.
"Does he like boys?"

Staring at his picture,
I wonder
how long
before I can leave
this place
and smile in a photo
like him? Or with him,
holding his hand.

Can I hang on?

Can this spinning blue light
save me until then?

ABBA-1975

Abba's lyrics, like water
shot from *La Bufadora*,
mingle with volcanic steam
from metallic pots of corn.

And the scrape on my knee
from chasing the seagulls
bleeds, but does not hurt.

On this Sunday, the ocean breeze slips
in gossip between vendor stalls
as young men in speedos walk past.
Tables of silver bracelets tap my eyes
and ABBA's Spanish melody
carries on my tongue
long before any English syllable
arrived. Before the summer ended
when it tore me
from the sands of Ensenada
to a desert north of the border,
to a land with tongues
unfamiliar and stiff.

And now when I fall,
chasing my shadow, my ABBA
lyrics cannot permeate
foreign soil. Cannot stop the pain.

The Knives Are Out

A mile from the border, my breath curls
like truck exhaust. the air smells of manure.
Across the railroad tracks, the school sits
next to the methadone clinic,
while the lettuce is harvested
two blocks away.

BMWs flood the parking lot. Watches of gold sparkle.
Plaid skirts swish, punctuated by *"Ay, que padre."* *

My arms folded, eyes scanning
Orwell's *1984*
looking for a way out. the chain link gate scrapes,
scratches, and puts up a good fight.

Plaid skirts, en masse,
razor edges slit
kindness like soft flesh
and behead the Virgin.

Smiles, faces caked like clowns,
scythes on silent saddle shoes
with tongues that will lash any church,
and dethrone any pope.

Nuns in black drag totter, e
yes submerged in waves of plaid.
Nervous hands break the surface. Rosary beads spill.

And *Jesucristo* nailed on the crucifix knows this.
Knows that when the plaid flutters
in the cold morning air,
when black drag surrenders,
He knows that the knives are out.

* "How cool" (Mexican Spanish)

Poplar Street

Poplar Street cuts
at an angle, like a midrib
on a leaf.

Baptized as the Boulevard
of Hollywood, its stars lie
unconscious on concrete reels.

On Poplar, the holy spirit rises at 420
and spills like rancid baby formula on
a chalk outline, blessing silhouettes
where high heels pivot.

On Poplar, where emerald crowns will never reign,
ramshackle cars drag race, shopping carts rattle,
despondent polka music thumps.

Voices call out, "Who is the father
of this baby?" Throats scream
that the air has eyes.

But no rustling, no gentle dances of leaves,
no caresses of sliding bodies of chlorophyll
sunbathing in a gentle canopy.

That is not Poplar Street.

Our Lady of the EBT

In San Diego,
tears run down the face
of a woman

on a mural
of a corner "market"
where holy candles
twirl in red and blue.

Where the EBT light spills
onto the body and blood
of a darker skinned Christ
and Our Lady weeps
while the cash register rings.

Where politicians bear false witness,
"I get things done."
And Our Lady gives them the finger
because drugs still dance between hands.

Where God's sheep look away,
fingers in ears
singing their hymns,
while little mouths
can see the tears
as the EBT sings.

Middle Age Magic

It's not magic
that I spin every day.
I spin something that looks like it.
But it's really the coffee
that keeps me going.

The magic died long ago,
but no one noticed.
And I pretended not to pay attention.

It's past midnight.
My husband is asleep.
I'm watching TV
without sex to keep us together.

I think I have time to write tomorrow.
But even so, the magic is gone.
It left long ago.
Sometimes, spurts of inspiration
maybe to start my own company
but I'm fifty, so it doesn't matter.

Did I tell you that the other day
I spun magic in an office meeting?
But it came out as an incoherent sentence.
And the millennials, these kids,
were about to get me a diaper
and sit me in a corner
because they could tell that the magic was gone.

There are no words, thoughts, or emotions
where I care. Not here. Not in this place
of spreadsheets, of mediocrity, of asinine requests
of attempts to pretend that something,
anything matters.

The magic is gone
and it's not coming back
unless one of these kids tells me that it's there,
Then, maybe, it will be okay.

Did I tell you that I can spin magic?
It's true.
Really, it is.

When the Revolution Never Happened

The revolution never happened.

shackled to one-eye prophets,
these revolutionaries
populated spreadsheets

like wizards
in towers
of stacked boxes.
in fishbowls
of steel and glass,
teased with sunlight.

tapping on keyboards
numbers, letters, symbols
pouring into empty cells
to look like scrolls,
to look like power,
to look like revolution.

Their overlords repeating
these incantations
to tell more tales,
to conjure more spells,
to keep the status quo.

Hitting the print button
the shackles remain,
the sunlight evaporates.

Revolutionaries can never
cast spells for others.
That's not how magic runs.
That's not how revolutions are made.

Saturday Morning

Someone's checkered bag sits
on the dusty concrete. Its ends unraveled
like my patience.

These frayed plastic strings
like your bleached blond hair
draped on cheeks of soft earth,
a peaked nose, with lips of Revlon.

I, painted in pinstripes
from this border fence
that follows me
like the church altar.

While cologne from last night's embrace
is woven into my shirt,
repeated in my morning
confession to God.

And yet, I stand in line to return to you.

Three bodies ahead,
a pink Aeropostale tee shirt
once on a young northerner,
screams and curses, its threadlike fingers
straining to keep its cargo intact.

And still before me,
strings of plastic hair
interlocked into a checkered bag,
like plastic words tied
into tasteless, translucent
kisses
I have promised to you.

Tirana

In Tirana,
friends walk in four-packs
men, young men
laughing, talking

Cafes waft with coffee.
Busses churn, cars swerve.
Footsteps turn, gaits stride.

The opera house, stone-faced
guards the people's mosaic,
figures marching,
banners high, proclaiming
the strength of Albania.

But on a dark side street,
sits a young man
who does not walk in four-packs,
who does not walk.

He sits in a wheelchair
with a cotton cap on his lap
unable to speak
unable to move his hands properly.

I see him
but just nod my head
pretending that's enough.

Cars swerve.
People jostle.

Weaving in and out,
across boulevards.

Stepping forward
on stairs
to restaurants,
to nightclubs.

Music playing.
Lights flashing.
Glasses clinking.

And in silence,
he sits patiently
for coins to drop
in a cotton cap.

I drop a coin
careful not to touch
his hand.

He tries to speak,
but his muscles
do not give him permission.

And I wish I could change
it for him. That I wasn't
so scared.

He looks up,
but his thoughts
do not become words.

He can only watch the world.

Maybe to travel
in a four-pack,
and swerve through
the streets
cigarette in hand,
moving forward,
step-by-step,
smiling, speaking.

Not Quite Heaven

I didn't make it to heaven.
There wasn't enough room
and my credit score was too low.

But I made it to the Heights.

Sitting in a purgatory of chain link,
below strands of lights
slouched on eaves,
I wait.

There's a pink church
on the corner and I wonder why
it's even needed.
But then the gunshots
tell me why.

There's a couch on a porch,
plastic toys strung out
on patches of dirt.
A car jacked up on cinder blocks
makes it clear that even Heaven
has given up on this place.

When my number is called,
the angels shake their heads.
"You're way ahead of schedule."
And I mumble, "This wasn't my idea."

But still, the chain-link gate does not open.
San Pedro is on a break. He's got the key.
And he just went union last year.

So, I watch the crabgrass lodged
between words of prayer. A blight
made worse by the donut marks
in the street.

I can't get a good night's sleep here.
Voices scream, the rattle
of recyclables shakes the earth.
Streets touched by faint moonlight
save for a neon sign "Cigarettes and Beer"
as lottery tickets flutter out the door.

Where the angels skulk and swagger
as I roll up my windows and lock my door.
Wrought iron fences keep out shadows
collapsed on sidewalks.

God says it's enough to have the stars light the streets.
There's no money in the budget this year.
But his stone and glass tower shines in the distance,
and I wonder why I even bother.

My friend got sick here, in the Heights.
The bank took the house. And the angels...
...well, they switched the locks.

Rainchecks are for Gamblers

Rainchecks are for gamblers
who think
there will be another hand
to play, on another day.
That there will be
other days.

For visiting friends. For road trips
that live in draft emails
because you think time
is a clatter of chips
cascading endlessly
into your hands.

You stack your days.

Bright lights dance above
the roulette spinning, spending
precious minutes,
hours,
days.

Dogeared, wrinkled rainchecks
sit in your pocket.

Move them to the center.
Bet your entire fortune.
Show your hand.

Alas, the house just folded.

Butrint

This Roman city, the valve
of the Ionian, once a fortress.
Its remnants, its Greek columns
line the winding walkways.

Storyboards sit and wait
to tell of the Byzantines,
of Ali Pasha.

But the real story
is in the dirt parking lot
where a young Syrian refugee
sells bracelets to tourists.

He approaches me.
"I do not need a bracelet" I tell him.
But he signals to his stomach.

"Where from?" he asks.
"California," I respond.
"America," he says.
"Viva, America," with a smile.

I fiddle in my pocket and drop
one euro in his hand. I point
to my wrist and wave "no".

And if it could only be different.
All of it.

So, he could enjoy life with friends,
to be worried, not about survival,
but about how many beers he will have.

And I, with my first-world guilt,
walk to a nearby bar
and drink
and watch him from afar
as he stands,
as he points to his stomach, waiting
for something to change.

Dystopia Threatened

The sun
hangs
at
an angle.
A mirror,
on its hinge,
askew-
falls,
breaks.
The earth
shifts.

.

5th Grade

I held his hand
by accident.

It was a windy day at lunch time
and the moment seemed right
when my hand fell into his.

For some reason,
he didn't let go
on our walk back
from the cafeteria.

Humberto. He was here,
sometimes. His family migrated
with the seasons. Sometimes
I walked alone.

He was my best friend. I didn't know
I could think of him another way,
that I could love him another way,
that there was even
a way.

And when we held hands
it felt like God had finished playing his game.
And I had won.

Like I could breathe,
even in this desert heat,
holding hands,
hoping no one would notice.

Tunnel of Miracles

The concrete walkway herds us
on dry rivulets that flow with tears
from yesterday's footsteps.
While the pharmacy pricks
miracles in a concrete tunnel.

Car exhaust wafts past the music notes
of a lost accordion. A child hops
wearing a Batman tee-shirt and I wonder
if someone will save me from this.

A fresh haircut. Tight, black spiky hair.
He holds hands with a dyed blond, a pink plastic
clip bundles splintered, burned locks. And I think
he can do better.

Plastic toys hang from banners.
In real cowboy hats, elderly *paleteros**
sell a cornucopia of frozen fruit.

An odor of sulphur cleanses me
of last night's sins. Shiny curves on plastic cars,
anorexic dolls with first world shame
sell their distortions in mirrors that laugh.
I pick up a Superman tee shirt,
and like a child, I fly away.

*paletero (Spanish)-ice cream man

One Note

This street has one note.
Its beat taps on angry tongues.
Its tempo thuds in cars of glue and tape.
Its chorus of blackbirds propels overhead.

By day, it drives
tree branches to suicide,
where birds flee to stunted vistas,
and poppies pull out their roots
to seek sanctuary in mediocrity.

By night,
this one note
embraces
unlit streets,
ugly liquor stores,
auto shops circled
in barbed wire
of gunfire.

Its churches praise it at 4:20,
with the body of Christ in one hand,
and a bong in the other.

This street is short on vision,
and long
on
this
one damn note.

Trashy Saint

He approaches the altar
and swipes the chalice
because God has the day off
but miracles still need to happen.

Outside, smoking a joint,
he waits at the curb for his ride,
scowling at businessmen,
scratching his balls.

His stubble is thick
and he counts the wrinkled bills
won in last night's bet.
The shadow from his red cap
softens his eye to a muted purple.

His ride cruises up the street.
Cobalt Blue. Heavy rims.
With an airplane engine
thrusting the car up,
like a parishioner
pleading to God.

The scantily clad woman
painted on the hood as a reminder
that even saints are human.

There are miracles to perform today
that only Freon and a wrench
can do. what a chalice cannot, what a prayer
can only pretend to touch.

His fingers release the empty cup,
falling like a lotto ticket
whose numbers mean nothing to no one.

Saint Cecilia

Waiting in the vestibule,
the ruby-red light
fills the chamber.

You enter. pulling
open wounds
with quiet footsteps.

Tears etch the lines
on your face. your scowl
grows, your grip
on the trigger
tightens.

Kneeling here,
so far from home,
I know that you have given up.
That your rage consumes you,
that your faults taunt you,
living like bullets lodged in your mind.

While your despot-loving parents
are too crazy, even for me,
to handle at times.
Now grab a hold of my hand
and let the sadness roar
out of your chest,
so that my love
casts itself into you.

Let my eyes take your sins,
so that I may taste them,
eat them, chew on them
for a little while and spin
them into magic
to remind you
that your divinity can be broken,
it can be flawed,
but it is still magical.

The Holy Ghost Ate the Stars

The Holy Ghost ate the stars.
Pulled them, plucked them from the blue sky
and crunched them like Funyuns from a 7-11.

Licking its fingers, it tossed their bones to street dogs.

For this was a Holy Ghost unlike any other,
a two-dimensional apparition
who held the word of God by its legs,
and discarded it like a candy wrapper
at a Wal-Mart parking lot.

It swore there was a problem,
that secret Santas sold children as furniture pieces,
that space lasers lit the planet like a barbecue,
that Sleestacks from *Land of the Lost*
were our neighbors.

And its cup must runneth over at 4:20,
for its hand is in the cookie jar, fire ants scaling it,
swarming, ravenous.

This is a Holy Ghost that I do not recognize,
for it incinerates the stars into a blanket of ash.

And behind its curtain of secrecy, it drops more digits.
While I, faithfully, turn mine up.

The Smashing Pumpkins

In the summer of 1992,
he hauled crates, plastic crates
of vinyl deities
when flyers were tweets,
when girlfriends were mandatory,
and a plague was devouring boys in the closet.

Outside of town, off the old highway
he played records on public radio.

Alternative music, they called it.
And it danced in a desert heat
that just would not quit.

Holding my head in my hands, sitting
next to dandelions that didn't know
any better, I mouthed the lyrics into the darkness,
while the pungent odor of the onion fields
insisted I was still alive.

And so, at 2am, he spun these records,
old records, new records
wondering if anyone was even listening.
And I, heartbroken, melancholy over a boy
learned to love the Smashing Pumpkins.

Dystopia Fights Back

mediocrity
swells.
its tongue
paints
a future to fear
with
its backwards,
its forwards
of images,
of reflections
in this house of mirrors.

And it laughs,
as you
hit a dead end,
and then another.
It calls
others
to join,
to mimic,
to mock
as you cry in fear.

Hollywood Boulevard

Light falls on a movie reel,
on a story that goes nowhere,
on Hollywood Boulevard
not in Hollywood, not a boulevard.

the story rises and falls
each night. fame finds a
new star ringed in chalk.

birds whirl
without nesting.

Our Lady of the EBT,
on the corner market wall.
a tear runs down her face,
while red and blue lights
flicker.

Empty spirits reflect
the liquor store marquee,
and the story begins again.

Monday Morning Meeting

cheap baubles jingle
in the hallway
like a cow crossing a road
about to be hit by a truck

the coffee
percolates, drips,
stops.

the hand
on the clock
stays still.

the printer
spits paper,
worth more
without words.

but it's those eyelashes
of tattered glass,
that run up and down
that make the day
into night.

their venom steeps in
the office corner
before the calvary,
the coffee
arrives.

they pierce my breath.
i fade into complicity.

batting those eyelashes
of glass, sharp and witty
slicing an artery

and they kill the hope
that I will ever leave.

Time to Think

A Bart Simpson piggy bank bobs past.
The desert sun sears my lip, my right ear and chin
while the shadows of the fence slice me.

I take two steps but would rather turn around.

Ahead, polyester arms folded. Bags colored, weaved
in plastic. Backs ache.
The line moves. Then stops.

Car exhaust. Rap music grates my ears, profanity
silences the melancholy yearning
of a *ranchera* ballad. Tires turn clockwise,
one minute, then another.

The bells ring on a cart with roses
of *Mazapan*. Cotton candy perched on sticks
like clouds from yesterday's sunset,
and hand-woven blankets sit
on the shoulder of a child.

Sweat trickles like tears from last night's confession
when my beard rubbed against yours. Your cologne on
my shirt. My foot moves forward and then back.
Someone cut in line.

Like a ghost, the *elotero* disappears
by the park. The trees, the crabgrass
locked in. And I
put the ring back on my finger.

Nine Knuckleheads

There's a southern seaport
led by knuckleheads,
nine knuckleheads to be exact,
who reside in a stone and glass tower.

As light and shadow clash over the city,
tents blossom like poppies
while little castles cling
to teetering hillsides,
their reservoirs empty,
their foundations buckling.

An army of shopping carts
brim with bicycle parts
reflects the sunlight like tiny stars
where Merlins gone mad
pop up apothecaries
to spin spells of addiction.

Glaring at the city,
their thrones turn, creak
while little kings
of little castles
devour one another.

Bomb Cyclone

The bomb cyclone
sliced the cold
spring air splintering
the edge
of town.

Still, no one heard it.
No one saw it coming.

For this bomb cyclone was different.

It would not dare enter
yet. It coiled and churned.

In steel grey,
it dropped rain like fingers
tapping,
waiting,
until
it
fell

on Main Street. A dollar flew
from Mr. Greyson's wallet
as quarters and nickels
broke windows
pulled high into the cold mass
and the winds harvested souls
that evaporated into the clouds.

The bomb cyclone had arrived.

The townspeople
drawn by its stardust glow,
blinded by its promises of jobs
threw themselves
on its throbbing check out machines.
With every beep a tighter grip.

And they could not stop.

Their roots naked, exposed,
dying, they could not stand
together like the prairie grasses
once had outside
the foreclosed family farms.

The bomb cyclone festered.
It exploded,
cascaded with discounts
of cheap, plastic trinkets
tumbling through manicured aisles.
waves of hair gel,
a sea of hand lotion,
an ice-cold flood of milk.

Pills for the sleepless.
Desserts for the hopeless.
Cigarettes for the jobless
with soft pillows to wait out the storm in aisle 6.

It offered boxes of dry pancake mix
and broken bits of Christmas garland
made by the hands of children
in another land, children
who also went hungry.

The bomb cyclone
crossed thresholds
in plastic bags heavy
with empty calories
and extra-long receipts.

It sat in living rooms uninvited
on curlicue chairs. It ate
at the dinner table
yammering in tasteless bits
of frozen corn, Velveeta slices, and sucrose pies.

It mumbled in bedrooms
through blinking images
in cheap picture boxes.

The bomb cyclone embraced
the town, stood behind it
Monday through Sunday
in births and deaths
squeezed its lungs,
till only it lived.
Tilted doorways in open fields
stared helplessly through overgrown grass.

The bakery shuttered.
The hardware store collapsed.
The shoe cobbler went without souls.

And what was left were blue vests
draped on tired bodies
propped up on arthritic knees
pushing metal carts
in an endless maze
of asphalt.

And as the sun appeared
in the cold spring air
not a cloud moved,
not a breath remained.

Heterosexual Dictatorship

It was never my dream to have a son.
Nor my father's.
And my grandfather did not dream.

I fester in the waters of regret,
rowing with two beer bottles
while my father, on auto play, fills it
with his words.

And in the evenings, when my longing
cannot be quenched,
when alcohol cannot kill desire,
the photographs on the walls weep
as brick-a-brac fly across the room,
waving goodbye for the last time.

My son looks the other way,
covers his ears,
and sees the photographs,
the people sobbing on the floor,
broken figurines at their feet.

And I dream
of brick-a-brac that never dies,
of photos with smiling faces,
and rooms without water.

I've Lost All My Tread

At the wheel,
the driver has fallen asleep.
And I, in the passenger seat,
lunge for the ignition key.

From the back,
your tongue, your cacophony
of how bad things are,
presses on the accelerator.

I listen to your dirges
grow louder,
whose songs,
whose rhythms of fear
have San Cristobal scrambling
off the dashboard.

The car swerves
to the far right,
to a cliff,

and this fuckin' seat belt
won't release!

The thinning hair
on my head,
these splinters
of tread,
cannot protect me.

The wall closes in.

I tug at the door
jammed,
locked,
with memories.

My arms cross over
my face. I shut
my eyes.

Dystopia Collapses

the end of an empire.

this house
of false
images,

mirrors
tilting,
teetering,

abandoned on the floor.

your fears
scrambling.
the terror
in their eyes.

they've lost their grip
on these mirrors.
the ones
they spun, recycled
into the old and the new.

Stand firm.

Hold one high.

And watch your fears die of absolute horror.

When Saturn Came Home

He knew I could no longer live in my skin.
My feelings for the body, for the soul of that boy
forced Saturn to descend from the heavens.

But when Saturn tried to come home
on that June night
he got detained at the border,
rescuing my heart from a boy
who had held it in a *Loteria* card,
and who, with his eyes closed, lost it in a wager.

And seeing no other way, Saturn found an opening
in the fence, hid his brilliance,
and tumbled into my backyard.

In his embrace, my face
pressed against his warm chest,
quenching his loneliness
with my tears. He lifted my head,
tending to my broken rings, their ends
had seared the earth.
While his breath deflected the shrill voices
who claimed dominion over the holy cosmos.

His hand reached for my fingers
for he needed me just as much
as I needed him. He hurled parts of his rings

to dance, to circle, and protect me
until I could ascend the heavens on my own,
until my skin was no longer alien to me.

And with that, Saturn sat with me in the darkness.
Not letting go, he held me as I sobbed,
so I would not collapse into the earth,
so that my world became mine again.

Beer Bottles from the Stars

The cigarette smoke marries
the desert heat, the stars
sit and drink, dropping
beer bottles

that litter the yard like constellations,
but more like receipts
for things we don't own,
but have already used.

The bottles lie half- empty
like courage that cannot speak
to tell my father that I am in love with a man.

The cicadas buzz, cling
to the mulberry trees
looking west beyond mountains,
to a coast that can't be seen.

And the bottles keep dropping
because it's too hot and hopeless,
even for the stars.

The cicadas stop singing.
The stars pause in mid-air.

A bottle drops.
I pick up my courage,
half empty on the floor,
to say what needs to be said.

A Prague Spring

A Prague Spring came to the office
one day, it sauntered in
with a casual look,
wearing a cotton checkered jacket,
and without coffee,
answered the phone
proclaiming,
"This mission statement is a real limp dick."

When Jesus Left Me at the Altar

"Forget it. This isn't going to work."
And with that, Jesus released my hand.

I turned to the congregation.
These last one hundred years,
of metallic memories
in shadow and light,
these gay men sitting
in suits of aluminum chiffon
that gleamed when
something funny came to mind.

I stood
in kaleidoscope color,
in darkness,
waiting,
but he never returned.

I descended the altar, past
the twinkling chiffon, past the murmurs,
past the oak door and opened my eyes
to the angelic sun.

I slipped the ring on my finger
and I promised to never settle,
to date lots of men, to travel
to foreign lands permeated
with cologne, cheap
pick-up lines, and beer.

This was the best thing
that could have happened,
when Jesus left me at the altar.

That Ford Escort

There's a Ford Escort that survived
the recession, when people had no choice
but to sell a part of themselves.

And this Ford Escort saved me,
loved me, when I could not accept, would not believe
that the touch of a strong hand
would make everything more than okay.

He accepted my singing, my crying, my promises
of something more. Candy wrappers, Styrofoam
containers, popcorn, sprinkled excuses that someday
we'd get out of here, beyond these pawn shops
and treeless streets.

His grey, rusted brown, metallic mange coat
stained, torn, holding it together for both of us.

He ran on K-Mart wages and $5.00 of gas
anticipating something beyond this place.

And he broke down only when I didn't,
when it was finally safe to do so,
when he knew I could save us both
on Interstate 10, fleeing parental love
that did not match its blue book value.

Ivory Towers

May your poetic words break down the doors
of these ivory towers, dethrone all the gods
of writing and slay its earthbound lieutenants.

May your poetic feelings feed the heart,
and revolt against the self-appointed generals
who look down on the quickie mart,
for that is where poetry truly lives:
at the checkout counter,
at the loading dock, on the couch of an apartment
in a shit neighborhood.

May your poetry eclipse
these towers. Destabilize them.
Drive your narrative to blast
the foundation, so that the rubble, the rabble
rumble into these towers
and topple them to the ground.

May your poetic words
haunt and torture
your fears, so they cannot outrun
your truth. for there is still one
more tower
that must collapse.

These Words

All good dictators
love you. to conform
in lockstep. to stand
for symbols. to fear.
to break

the first commandment,
to repeat, heart in hand
not your words.

But in the silence
bruises heal,
the voice strings syllables
until the conscience speaks.

And fear, like all good dictators,
will tremble at these words,
will collapse with heart in hand,
will stand on the precipice.

And in this rain,
the birds will tweet,
the chorus will rise,
and dictators will fall.

On the Street

Run naked through the streets
and shout,
"Make love to me!"

Tag every wall in a turf war
with quotes from the *paletero*,
from the child who yearns for love,
from the gay son who hopes his father
will welcome him,
this time.

With your sharp and fast tongue, mesmerize
passersby as they get caught
in the gunfire of stanzas and sonnets,
popping the air.

Bellow on the street corner
of how love abandoned you,
how your life is empty,
how you aborted your dreams.
And every day it rips into you
of every opportunity you threw away.

I want that on the wall.
I want all the pain and hurt
to get out of bed, to grab that bullhorn
and run naked through the streets.

Aftermath

In the quiet
of what was,
syllables will string
together
into song

Search through
the ashes
of these broken
words
to find them.

Rub them in,
breathe them in.
And in your breath,
of these consonants,
of these vowels,
is the way forward.

Abandon the "O"

The whimpering, the howling would not stop.
My grandfather had abandoned his faithful "O".

When the foreman called for "Richard",
my grandfather raised his hand
when Mexicans could not be Mexican.
When separate theatres and
separate swimming days
separated brown and white bodies.

When Ricardo became Richard,
he evaporated into the light-skin background
of little box homes, leaving "O" on the street
like a dog, to fend for itself, to die
in the desert cold,
beyond the manicured green lawns.

And now,
years after "Richard" dissolved,
I'm told, "Play the game. Drop the O.
Leave it like your grandfather's dog.
It will learn to limp along."
But I would rather burn
down such a closet.

I stand outside
and pick up my grandfather's "O"
by the embers of his past,
malnourished and shivering,
unable to speak.

It Felt Like a Wednesday

It felt like a Wednesday
when those mountains
got in the way.

At the Greyhound Station,
behind the Foster's Freeze,
is where I saw you last,
on that Wednesday.

Where dreams sit on asphalt, waiting
for a handout. where Russian thistle tumbles
on flat streets, on slabs of concrete
without your shadow to comfort my eyes.

Someone said they saw you in a polaroid,
in the mass of faces waiting at the border,
in a grainy picture in the local paper.

My thoughts pick up speed,
spinning, swirling like that dust devil,
turning, turning
into
nothing.

I surrendered
my spirit in this parking lot,
and my will was sold
at auction to the highest bidder.

But I swear, I saw you
in that phone booth,
in that car,
at that party.
and for a moment,
it felt like a Wednesday.

Halfway

Before my footsteps, the light
splinters, retreats
into a dark corner.

High above, he curses
rusted nails.

And finally,
letting go,
falls
onto the tiled floor.

"Why the hell
am I up so high, anyway?"

He looks tired and dirty,
and would be suspicious
in a nice white neighborhood.

The pew creaks when he sits.
He lays his hand
on my shoulder, but I shrug
and move away.

Glancing at the cross, he turns to me.

"You want me to get up there?"
I shake my head in disbelief.

His fingers interlocked,
his feet fidgeting.
"You already are."

And as I pull out each memory,
my face writhes in pain,
as each mistake clatters onto the floor.

His eyes downcast,
he places one hand
between us.

And this time,
I meet him halfway.

Tepelenë

The waters of Tepelenë splash
into a stone fountain, to offer redemption
to the kneeling maple tree
who, confessing its sins, drops them
onto the mist-soaked soil.

I climb the stairs. past
the waterfall. Its droplets
soothe my tough, thick skin.

In the open-air café,
I order the house special
and observe from a tree branch.

Under the humble canopy, a goat on its forelegs
nibbles on leaves

resting on a red chair. An elderly man
sells jars of honey.

I listen to the water running.
The bathroom faucet does not
have an off switch,
as clear, fresh redemption
is washed away,
without sins spinning into the drain,
without the release of regrets.

I swirl, turn, and mix
the fresh yogurt in the white bowl,
the honey and nuts thicken
like a salve, a spoonful
renews my courage.

Downstairs, I kneel
before the fountain
to wash away my fears,
and I release my sins
to die at my feet.

*A town in southern Albania famous for its natural
springs

The Dairy Mart

An overhang faces
a brick highway. Its rusted edges,
like the red and orange sky
like a flock of birds
doused in neon light
where trucks and men travel,
eyes grimed in dust.

We grabbed a burger here
at the Dairy Mart
in your 49' Ford pickup
before the war,
when my hair was jet black
and yours sunny blond.

You kissed me in the open air.

Your hand on my lower back,
your beard against my chin
as our lips touched.
Your tongue enveloped my mouth
scented with ketchup,
salt crystals on my cheek.

My eyes watched the road
to make sure no one was coming for us.

I leaned into you, immersed in burnt light
our shadows held each other,
indiscernible, melded into the air.

But the war in Korea ended it all.
And I never knew what became of you.
After the salty kiss,
after the war was done.

I wanted to tell you
that I had waited,
that your kiss lived
in my shirt pocket
listening to me live.

I closed my eyes and saw you
in mirrored reflections of memory.

In a salty kiss and firm embrace
of pick-up rides and burnt clouds
swirled, catapulted, and smashed
into an envelope. Returned,
unopened.

Touching my shirt pocket,
I wonder where you are,
whom do you love,
whose shadow do you share?

The Madonna

The Material Girl rolls across the floor
smashing the border fence
right into Colonia Esperanza*
where a cute boy lives near the foam
of the New River.

Where the gay drag bar hovers
on its banks, the cement foundation juts
over the edge. an impersonator lip syncs,
twirling her rosary.

Where the bus dies in the middle
of the street on a desert mid-day
searching for my boy, and his brother
died of TB, the next.

Where a car radio blares "Like a Virgin"
while the *paletero** rings his bell
for another soul has made it to heaven.

Where a motel has all its rooms unlocked.
And we spend an awkward night unfamiliar
with each other, while Our Lady watches.

And on a Sunday morning
the Madonna sits with us
while we eat *birria*,
under the tarp of a home
that has become a restaurant,
that the Material Girl rolled into.

*Colonia Esperanza- a neighborhood in Mexicali
*paletero- ice cream vendor

Geneva

In my mind Geneva sings
on the streets of San Diego
though I drank her melody but once
on the Nebraskan plain.

She croons on the city sidewalks
and hums in its piñata-swinging parks
the ones I seldom walk on or visit.

She serenades a bird on a decrepit wall
to bring hope
that as gun shots pop at night,
love and beauty
are still here,
somewhere, in this city.

But I grow impatient, thirsty
for fields of green,
for the ballad of the prairie
for the muse who lays lyrics
in my mind
like a plow
on the open plain.

When Geneva flows in ink
from my pen,
the notes like broken soil,
like bits of chaff and stover,
take flight.

Geneva plants the chorus,
and harmonizes the verse
on the vast, fertile page.

In the distance,
the outro billows,
Geneva's voice whispers,
beyond the grain silos,
beyond the waves,
somewhere
on the Nebraskan plain.

Utopia

No more contradictions
of mirrored images
in this fun house
of sadness,
of limitation.

A new world.
Unified
Free
of your own making,
dripping in song,
story,
lives under two skies.

break
the rearview mirror.
hit the gas pedal.

Till the Heart

Poetry tills the heart.
It softens it,
so that it never hardens,
so that it never breaks.

Tell me again
how do I find my love
whose voice spoke
in a book of happiness 800 years ago?

Shall I tell my friends that friendship
is overrated?
Shall I tell my mother that raising children
was not for her?
Shall I tell everyone who wants to, to run away
and leave a note, a stanza,
saying why they abandoned
this endless grind of minimum wage
and minimum hope
to search,
to live,
and
to love?

Then take that can of spray paint
and douse that wall with your nakedness,
bear your darkest secrets to public view
so that the monster of shame cannot hide.

The Streets of Tirana

Cars swing on the roundabout,
while pedestrians dart across the boulevard,
and buses weave between
bicycles and goodbyes.

Cafes lean on sidewalks.
Bakeries, crepes rise
in circles. Conversations dash
out onto the street
to catch a bus or meet a friend.

The double-headed eagle soars
as the bicyclist disappears
under the canopy of trees. I slow my pace,
and stop to nest on chairs perched
beside a café railing,
by the produce market,
past the old pyramid.

The hot, flaky *byrek* crumbles in bits
onto the floor
where birds hop to peck and chat.

Four packs of young men breeze past,
while hellos and coffee waft in the air,
and pine trees reveal the secrets of passersby.
Dripping in happiness, I take another bite.

Paper Twitter

Scrawled in heavy black ink.
Tacked to outdoor corkboards.
"For Hire" "Room for Rent" "Lonely and Bored?"
Before apps.
Before computers.

When buses, not planes,
moved you from here to there.
Sometimes,
forever.

When you ran to the TV to catch your television
show and your friend held the rabbit ears
standing on one leg, curling
tin foil on antennas
and you yelled,
"Move to the left! More! Keep going!"

When you scanned the phone book
to find his address. And rode your bike
by his house hoping to see him.

When your brother called
from the living room
because your favorite song
just came on the radio
and it might not happen again
for a couple of hours.

And still, you didn't have enough
to buy the single at the record shop,
so you pressed "record"
on your cassette player
with the radio next to it.

And texting was not an electronic verb,
but a paper noun.

When no one followed me.
when my friends were three-dimensional.
before tweets, likes, follows made for
a cascade of phantom connections.
And tik tok is what a clock did.

Road Trip

Near Alliance,
an old Chevy hummed
a new tune.

Like sandhill cranes, we folded
light into gray, past the rivers
of Platte and Wood.

Valentine, lovesick
in the back seat,
strummed a Broken Bow,
hitchhiking a ballad
to Grand Island.

Just then, my Alma flew past me
in a Buick no less,
laughing into the future
as our car buzzed
like a dragonfly to Riverton.

There, I sat on the sidewalk
waiting for the children to visit
the corner market, where a tree
now grows through the cash register.

Later that afternoon,
while in a Funk I admired
the Red Clouds over Blue Hill
and listened to a melody
floating in from Bladen.

With cassette tapes whirling tunes,
I swung by Hebron to pick up a Friend
and we met Beatrice in Steele City
who recited Kooser's poetry
all the way to Brownville,
to see Rudloff smile one more time.

But it was Lincoln, and then Omaha that pulled me
northward. When I kneeled
before St. Cecilia, someone who looked
like me trembled in the pew ahead.

Outside, Mason led his flock of bombers,
while in Bancroft, Neihardt wove dreams into stories
and in Gandy, Geneva serenaded from afar.

The Chevy and I said our goodbyes.
And I hiked along the waters of the Elkhorn,
to find the spirit of the Cowboy,
to find a new way home.

Sandia

In the winter of 1992,
in the middle of a lettuce field
I hold my suitcase
standing on splinters of a memory.

Where steel tracks once crossed,
green leaves flutter
in the quiet, in the stillness
while dragonflies float in the orange sky.

The bits of railroad ties
where Sandia once stood
are like black and white photos
of a past I can't remember.

But the train will come.

I lower my heaviness
to the soft earth. I tap my fingers
to a beat, breathing
slowly. Then, just then,
the train whistle pierces
the air, and my smile returns.

Amidst the locomotive steam,
my beloved holds me
on the platform. Not letting go,
I disappear,
into the evening,
into the darkness.

Mirupafshim

"*Mirupafshim*" he smiled, gripping my hand.

In the morning, I had seen him
sitting under the old pine.
Watching,
cigarette in hand
from his blue box bar
that one day will rest
in the waters, in the stories
of the Ionian.

He had seen many birthdays,
his dry rivulet skin, cascaded in shadows
like canyons the years had etched deep.

I wanted to know his story,
to listen and learn.
Whom had he loved?
And what had defeated him?

I wanted to ask him about Hoxha.*
Where had he found the strength?
Was it from the sea?

I approach him and smile.
In my broken Albanian
I stutter my words,
trying to tell my story,
"One coffee, please."

He nods.

And when I leave
I say, "*Mirupafshim.*"
He takes my hand in his
gripping tight, "*Mirupafshim*"
smiling, looking into my eyes
for the first
and for the last time.

And I become despondent
as I walk away,
for one day when I return
he will be gone.

But in the end,
we will sit together
under the old pine
by the Ioanian.

And he will share his story,
as tears flow down his cheeks,
as his words trickle into the sea,
without end, without goodbyes.

**Enver Hoxha (Communist dictator who ruled
Albania from 1945-1985)*

Time to Move On

Outside of Alliance,
in the fields of wheat
I found a Buick
perched on a pedestal.

And I figured that this
was the right time to run away.

He creaked and peeled,
tearing his prison sentence
into flakes of floating paint.

He waved to me.
"Hey, buddy. Can you give me a hand?"

I held out my arms
ready to catch him
as he clambered down.

I cleaned his headlights
covered in grey paint
so, he could see more
clearly, so I could see.

And he coughed when I turned the ignition key.

"Where to?" he asked.
"Let's just go." I replied.
"Till we run out of time."

I Wait for the Stars

Every night,
I see you
dance at the edge,
at the precipice
where the darkness is swallowed
by Gjirokastran stars,
drawing your silhouette.

These cobble stones,
these old memories,
of this old castle,
sing softly
when you tap them
to hum something new.

When night surrenders
to morning, the moon opens
its hand to release
my memory
of our night.

And so,
I wait for the stars
to cast your silhouette,
to dance with you
once again.

Bladen

When Geneva sang
on the streets of Bladen
no one stopped to listen
for there was no one left.

In the cold sunshine, Geneva
remembered the theatre.
Now boarded up,
Now doused with color
to hide its loneliness

Geneva sang every morning
to ward off
the humming of the dead,
of the ghosts pulling her closer
to the cemetery
beyond the grain silos.

And on an improvised number
she twirled, dipped, and stretched
to the music only she could hear.
For only she was alive.

And when she fell,
the dead called even louder.
Geneva paid them no mind.
She dusted off the fear
serenading

for the memories
of bugles on the 4th of July,
for the sounds of guitars
plucking on a Saturday night,
for the voices of past loves,
their shadows floating over
now silent streets
slipping through train tracks
to rest in fields of corn.

And when Geneva sang
on the streets of Bladen
the dead stopped to listen,
dancing into the memory of time.

Broadway & 9th

As I stand on the corner of
Broadway and 9th
the spotlight rolls overhead.

The cast of clouds move
the audience, their shadows
welcomed to the performance.

My voice rises,
my hands lift over the stage
of grass and goldenrod.

The crimson glow
commences the 2nd half.

The lights of heaven turn on.
And I am finally
among the stars.

For I did not find them
on the sidewalks of
Hollywood.

I found them
in the crisscross of wheat fields,
living in eaves, gables, and doorways,
in abandoned schools, stores, and
churches
where spirits still chatter, sing, and
applaud.

I did not find the stars in
the tall concrete shadows,
in the crawling cars
on tangled asphalt suspended
over cardboard camps,
under the orange sky.

I found them at the intersection
of quilts of wheat,
in the tips of bluestem and buffalo grass,
on the specks of dew drops.

I found the applause
in the curtains of trees
standing stoically,
promenading in place.

In the cornstalks stretching
their necks in the luminescence.
A captive audience
miles to the back row.

I did not find my voice in Hollywood,
on the surface of smoked glass
where everything lived.

Now when I sing,
the lines on my face cut sharply
as the plow on Nebraskan soil.

My eyes rest in the darkness,
my voice rises to the stars
as I stand on the corner of Broadway and 9th.

Two Skies

You can't find
Tirana, Gjirokastër, or Ksamil *
on a map of Nebraska.
But they are there.

When you drive off Interstate 80,
on the shoulders of your thoughts,
on the outskirts of your imagination,
you will reach a country road
that descends into a quiet village.

There you will live
under two skies that ripple
from the shores of Ksamil,
to the songs whispering
on the plains of Bladen.

You will sit on the wall of a fortress above
Gjirokastër, while the Platte River
counts its raindrops in the valley below.

In the quiet of the Antiquarium**
books with their stories await you.
And the youthful streets of Tirana,
where you walk to write your story.

Where Mount Dajti guards
the wheat fields of Red Cloud,
and the Niobrara River cascades
into the waterfalls of Tepelenë.

Where a coffee with Kadare and Kooser***
in Berat, collaborate with notes in hand.
And Willa Cather tags the castle walls
of Shkodra, looking north to the mountains of Theth.

Where the frenetic energy
of the Romans, Byzantines, and Ottomans
interweaves with the Czechs, the Bohemians.

And the richness appears,
of energy and solitude,
of waving grasses,
and mosaics of stone,
of cornstalks rustling like passengers
on a bus to Durres.

And the words carried by the winds
from Sarande to Gilead,
tell of legends.

If you stop to listen,
you will live under two skies.

* Cities in Albania famous for their history, natural beauty, and culture. This includes Tepelenë, Durres, Berat, Ksamil, Theth, and Sarande.

**Well-known bookstore once located in downtown Omaha, famous as a center of culture and community events.

***Ismail Kadare, internationally famous Albanian writer. Ted Kooser, former US Poet Laureate 2004-2006.

Acknowledgements

A big thank you to the following journals for publishing earlier versions of these poems:

Nebraska Writers Guild: Voices from the Plains Anthology, Vol. III: December 2019
"Bladen", "Geneva", and "Bomb Cyclone"

Nebraska Writers Guild: How It Looks from Here: Poetry from the Plains. (2019) "Broadway & 9th"

Verses from the Plains: A Poetry Collection. October 2020. "Road Trip"

Nebraska Writers Guild: Voices from the Plains Anthology, Vol. IV: December 2020

Diversity: There's a beauty in that too: A poetry collection. January 2021. "These Words"

Perceptions Magazine: June 2021 issue. "Tepelenë" and "Our Lady of the EBT."

San Diego Writers Ink: 2021 A Year in Ink Anthology. "When Jesus Left Me at the Altar"

Other Wordly Women Press: 2021 Summer Anthology. "Till the Heart"

Beatific Magazine: 2021 Fall Issue. "Beer Bottles from the Stars" and "Sandia"

The Seattle Star: April-2021. "The Madonna"

DASH Literary Journal: May 2021 Issue. "Heterosexual Dictatorship", "5th Grade", and "The Knives are Out"

Stirring: Summer 2021. Vol. 23 Ed. 3. "Abandon the 'O' "

Midwest Quarterly: Fall 2021 Issue. "Two Skies"

Brief Wilderness: October 2021. "Saturday Morning" & "Tunnel of Miracles"

Glint Literary Journal: December 2021, Issue 12. "The Holy Ghost Ate the Stars"

Nebraska Writers Guild: Voices from the Plains Anthology, Vol. V: December 2021 "Saint Cecilia" "Poplar Street" & "Time to Move On"

The Round (Brown University): January 2022-Issue XXII. "The Smashing Pumpkins"

Wrath-Bearing Tree: March 2022 Issue. "ABBA-1975" & "On the Street"

Evening Street Press & Review: 2022 Issue. "That Ford Escort" and "Paper Twitter"

Cider Press Review: March 2022 Issue. "Time to Think" *Slab* (Slippery Rock University): April 2022-Issue 17. "It Felt Like a Wednesday"

East Jasmine Review: September/October 2022. "Trashy Saint", "When Saturn Came Home", "One Note", "I've Lost All My Tread" & "Blue Light Special"

ABOUT THE AUTHOR

Ricardo Moran is a past recipient of the Peter K. Hixson Memorial Award for Poetry. His writing has been published in *Beatific Magazine, Midwest Quarterly, Perceptions Magazine, East Jasmine Review, The Seattle Star,* and *Willa Cather Review.* He is a member of the Nebraska Writers Guild; serves on the board of San Diego Writers Ink; and is an associate editor with Zoetic Press. He currently lives in Albania; enjoys traveling; and learning how to say "good morning" in as many languages as possible. In every timeline, you can find him reading, writing, and plotting right here: www.ricardomoranwriter.com